A History of World War II: as told by AI

Compiled by James Nyder

Pt 1939-1940

1939 was a year that marked the beginning of several significant events, both political and historical. The first half of the year saw the signing of the Molotov-Ribbentrop Pact, the first steps towards the outbreak of World War II, and the start of the Holocaust.

The Molotov-Ribbentrop Pact was a non-aggression treaty signed between the Soviet Union and Nazi Germany on August 23, 1939. The pact allowed for the two countries to divide Eastern Europe into spheres of influence, with the Soviet Union gaining control over Latvia, Estonia, Finland, and parts of Poland. The signing of the pact was seen as a betrayal by the Western powers, who had been trying to form an alliance with the Soviet Union in order to counter the threat of Nazi Germany.

In the months leading up to the signing of the Molotov-Ribbentrop Pact, Nazi Germany had been making aggressive moves towards Poland. In March 1939, Germany had invaded Czechoslovakia, annexed the western regions of Bohemia and Moravia, and created the Slovak Republic. In April, Germany threatened Poland with military action if it did not cede control of the Polish Corridor, a strip of land connecting Germany to its province of East Prussia.

On September 1, 1939, Nazi Germany invaded Poland, marking the official start of World War II. The invasion was met with a declaration of war by Britain and France, who were bound by treaty to defend Poland. The war would go on to last for six years and involve the majority of the world's nations, resulting in the deaths of millions of people.

Also in 1939, the Holocaust began with the invasion of Poland. The Holocaust was the systematic extermination of millions of Jews, along with other groups deemed undesirable by the Nazi regime, including Roma, disabled individuals, and homosexuals. The Holocaust would continue until 1945, resulting in the deaths of six million Jews and millions of others.

In summary, the first half of 1939 saw the signing of the Molotov-Ribbentrop Pact and the first steps towards the outbreak of World War II. The beginning of the Holocaust would also mark the start of one of the greatest atrocities in human history.

The first month of World War II was marked by a series of rapid and significant events that set the stage for the conflict to come. The war officially began on September 1, 1939, when Nazi Germany invaded Poland. In response, Britain and France declared war on Germany, marking the first time the two countries had gone to war against Germany since World War I.

In the days following the invasion of Poland, German forces made rapid progress, using a combination of ground forces and air power to overwhelm the Polish army. On September 9, Soviet forces invaded Poland from the east, further dividing the country and making it difficult for Polish forces to mount an effective defense.

On September 17, Poland officially surrendered to Germany, marking the end of the first major battle of World War II. The fall of Poland was followed by a period of occupation, as German and Soviet forces divided the country between them and began implementing policies aimed at repressing and exploiting the Polish people.

In the meantime, British and French forces were mobilizing for war, but were unable to offer significant support to Poland due to a lack of preparedness and inadequate military equipment. As the month ended, the two countries were engaged in a series of diplomatic efforts aimed at forming an alliance with the Soviet Union, in the hopes of countering the threat of Nazi Germany.

The first month of World War II saw the rapid invasion and occupation of Poland by German and Soviet forces. Britain and France declared war on

Germany but were unable to offer significant support to Poland due to a lack of preparedness. As the month ended, the two countries were engaged in diplomatic efforts aimed at forming an alliance with the Soviet Union.

The second month of World War II saw a continuation of the conflict that had begun with the invasion of Poland in September 1939. German and Soviet forces continued to occupy Poland, implementing policies aimed at repressing and exploiting the Polish people. In the meantime, British and French forces were mobilizing for war, but were unable to offer significant support to Poland due to a lack of preparedness and inadequate military equipment.

One of the key events of the second month of the war was the signing of the Molotov-Ribbentrop Pact on August 23, 1939. The pact was a non-aggression treaty between the Soviet Union and Nazi Germany, which allowed for the two countries to divide Eastern Europe into spheres of influence. The signing of the pact was seen as a betrayal by the Western powers, who had been trying to form an alliance with the Soviet Union in order to counter the threat of Nazi Germany.

The first half of 1940 was a crucial period for the course of World War II. During this time, several significant events took place that would have lasting impacts on the conflict.

One of the most notable events of the first half of 1940 was the invasion of Denmark and Norway by German forces. On April 9, 1940, German forces launched a surprise attack on Denmark, quickly overwhelming the country's small army and occupying the country within a few hours. On April 10, German forces invaded Norway, using a combination of ground forces and air power to secure control of the country.

The invasion of Denmark and Norway was a major setback for the Allies, who had been supporting the Norwegian government against the threat of Axis aggression. The fall of the two countries allowed German forces to establish a foothold in Scandinavia and put them in a strategic position to launch further attacks on the Allied powers.

In the meantime, British and French forces were struggling to respond to the German invasion of Norway. Despite initial attempts to provide support to the Norwegian government, the two countries were unable to prevent the German occupation of the country. As the first half of 1940 ended, the two countries were preparing for a possible invasion by German forces, as tensions continued to escalate in Europe.

In the Pacific Theater, the war between the United States and Japan continued to escalate. On January 27, 1940, the United States imposed an embargo on the export of iron, steel, and scrap metal to Japan, in an effort to curtail Japanese aggression in the region. The embargo was seen as an act of economic warfare against Japan and would prove to be a significant factor in the escalation of hostilities between the two countries.

The first half of 1940 was a crucial period for the course of World War II. The invasion of Denmark and Norway by German forces and the escalating tensions between the United States and Japan were major events of this period, as the conflict continued to spread and intensify.

This rapid advancement period of World War II saw the continuation of the conflict that had begun with the invasion of Poland in September 1939. The signing of the Molotov-Ribbentrop Pact and the invasion of Denmark and Norway by German forces were significant events of the month, as tensions continued to escalate in Europe. British and French forces were unable to offer significant support to Poland or Norway, due to a lack of preparedness and inadequate military equipment.

In America, the country was beginning to emerge from the Great Depression, and the economy was starting to improve. The United States was also preparing for the possibility of involvement in the ongoing conflict in Europe, as World War II raged on.

On the international front, the war continued to escalate, with major battles taking place in various parts of Europe and Africa. The Nazi regime in Germany expanded its control over much of Europe, and the Allied powers struggled to push back against the Axis powers.

As the Great Depression came to an end, the American economy began to improve. Unemployment rates declined, and many Americans found jobs in industries that were growing, such as manufacturing and construction. The government implemented policies to stimulate the economy, such as the New Deal programs, which provided relief to workers and businesses.

At the same time, the United States was watching the situation in Europe closely. World War II had been raging for several years, and the country was concerned about the possibility of being drawn into conflict. The government began to prepare for the possibility of war, including building up its military forces.

As the war continued to escalate, major battles took place in various parts of Europe and Africa. The Nazi regime in Germany, led by Adolf Hitler, expanded its control over much of the continent, and the Allied powers struggled to push back against the Axis powers. The war also spread to other parts of the world, including Asia and the Pacific.

In America, the government implemented a number of measures to support the war effort. One of the most significant was the formation of the Office of War Mobilization, which was responsible for coordinating the country's resources and manpower to support the war. The government also instituted the draft, requiring young men to register for military service.

In addition, the United States began to provide aid to the Allied powers, including supplying them with weapons and other military equipment. Many Americans also volunteered to serve in the military, and the country sent troops to Europe and other parts of the world to fight against the Axis powers. During the second half of 1940, the war in Europe continued to escalate. In June, Germany launched a massive invasion of the Soviet Union, in a campaign known as Operation Barbarossa. This was the largest military operation in history, involving more than three million German soldiers, as well as other Axis forces. The goal of the campaign was to defeat the Soviet Union and secure control of its vast resources.

Initially, the German invasion was successful, and the German forces quickly advanced deep into Soviet territory. However, the Soviet Union was able to mount a strong resistance, and the invasion eventually stalled. The harsh Russian winter also played a role, as it slowed the German advance and allowed the Soviet forces to regroup and counterattack.

The Soviet Union also received support from the Western Allies, including the United States. In July, the United States and the Soviet Union signed the Lend-Lease Act, which allowed the United States to provide military equipment and other supplies to the Soviet Union. This aid was crucial to the Soviet war effort, and it helped to turn the tide against the Axis powers.

In the Pacific theater, the war also continued to escalate. In December, the Japanese launched a surprise attack on the American naval base at Pearl Harbor, which marked the United States' official entry into the war. This attack was a major blow to the United States, as it destroyed much of the American Pacific fleet and killed thousands of American servicemen.

Following the attack on Pearl Harbor, the Japanese launched a series of offensives in the Pacific, including the conquest of the Philippines and other territories. The Japanese military was highly successful in these early campaigns, and it seemed that the war in the Pacific was going in their favor.

Overall, the second half of 1940 was a time of significant events and developments in the war. The conflict continued to spread and escalate, with major battles and campaigns taking place in various parts of the world. These events would have a profound impact on the course of the war and the future of the world.

Pt 2 1941 and Beyond

The period between January and February 1941 was a significant one for the course of World War II. During this time, several key events took place that would have lasting impacts on the conflict.

One of the most notable events of this period was the signing of the Lend-Lease Act by the United States Congress on March 11, 1941. The act allowed the United States to provide military aid to countries that were fighting against the Axis powers, including Britain and the Soviet Union. The Lend-Lease Act was seen as a major step towards American involvement in the war and would prove to be a crucial source of support for the Allied powers.

Another significant event of this period was the invasion of Greece by Axis forces, which began on April 6, 1941. German, Italian, and Bulgarian forces launched a coordinated attack on Greece, quickly overwhelming the country's small army and occupying the country within a few weeks. The invasion of Greece was a major setback for the Allies, who had been supporting the Greek government against the threat of Axis aggression.

In the Pacific Theater, the war between the United States and Japan continued to escalate. On February 19, 1941, the United States announced the freezing of Japanese assets, which was seen as an act of economic warfare against Japan. In response, Japan intensified its efforts to expand its empire in the Pacific, invading British and Dutch territories in the region.

In 1941, the world was engulfed in the deadliest conflict in human history: World War II. The war had begun in 1939, when Germany, under the leadership of Adolf Hitler, invaded Poland. Since then, the conflict has spread across Europe, into Africa and the Middle East, and across the Pacific to Asia.

In 1941, several major events occurred that would shape the course of the war. In April, Germany invaded Yugoslavia and Greece, quickly conquering both countries. This expansion of German territory in the Balkans gave them access to important resources such as oil and minerals.

In May, the German battleship Bismarck was sunk in the Atlantic Ocean by British forces, dealing a major blow to the German navy. The loss of the Bismarck was a significant setback for Germany and reduced their ability to project power at sea.

In June, Hitler launched a massive invasion of the Soviet Union, known as Operation Barbarossa. The goal of the invasion was to quickly defeat the Soviet Union and gain control of its vast territories and resources. Despite initial successes, the invasion quickly stalled, and the Germans were unable to achieve a decisive victory. The Soviet Union proved to be a formidable opponent, with vast territories and a large and determined army. The failure of Operation Barbarossa was a major setback for Germany and marked the beginning of the end of their military dominance.

In the Pacific, Japan continued its expansion, attacking and occupying British and Dutch colonies in Southeast Asia. This brought Japan into conflict with the Western powers and increased tensions in the region. In December, Japan launched a surprise attack on the United States naval base at Pearl Harbor, drawing the US into the war.

In the United States, President Franklin D. Roosevelt declared war on Japan and began mobilizing the country for war. The US also provided aid to the Soviet Union, helping them to resist the German invasion.

In 1941, the war was at a critical juncture, with battles raging on multiple fronts and the outcome still uncertain.

In 1941, the world of science was abuzz with excitement and discovery. One of the most significant events of the year was the publication of the paper "The Structure of DNA" by James Watson and Francis Crick. This groundbreaking research, published in the journal Nature, described the discovery of the double helix structure of DNA, which was a major breakthrough in our understanding of genetics and the transmission of inherited traits.

Another important event in 1941 was the discovery of the chemical element Astatine. This heavy, radioactive element, discovered by Corson, Mackenzie, and Segrè, was the heaviest of the halogen elements and added to our understanding of the periodic table.

Additionally, 1941 saw the successful use of penicillin as an antibiotic, marking a significant milestone in the treatment of bacterial infections. This discovery paved the way for further research into the use of antibiotics to combat disease.

In April 1941, several significant events occurred that would shape the course of history.

On April 6, Germany invaded Yugoslavia and Greece, quickly conquering both countries. This expansion of German territory in the Balkans gave them access to important resources such as oil and minerals.

On April 14, the British commando raid on the Lofoten Islands in Norway took place. This was a successful operation that destroyed several factories producing fish oil and glycerin for the German war effort.

On April 18, the United States officially ended its Neutrality Act, allowing it to sell weapons to the Allied powers. This was a significant shift in US policy and marked the country's increasing involvement in the war.

On April 27, the German concentration camp at Auschwitz-Birkenau was opened in Poland. Over the next several years, millions of Jews, Roma, and others deemed undesirable by the Nazi regime would be imprisoned and killed at Auschwitz.

In the months of May through August 1941, several significant events occurred that would shape the course of World War II.

In May, the German battleship Bismarck was sunk in the Atlantic Ocean by British forces, dealing a major blow to the German navy. The loss of the Bismarck was a significant setback for Germany and reduced their ability to project power at sea.

In June, Hitler launched a massive invasion of the Soviet Union, known as Operation Barbarossa. The goal of the invasion was to quickly defeat the Soviet Union and gain control of its vast territories and resources. Despite initial successes, the invasion quickly stalled, and the Germans were unable to achieve a decisive victory. The Soviet Union proved to be a formidable opponent, with vast territories and a large and determined army. The failure of Operation Barbarossa was a major setback for Germany and marked the beginning of the end of their military dominance.

In the Pacific, Japan continued its expansion, attacking and occupying British and Dutch colonies in Southeast Asia. This brought Japan into conflict with the Western powers and increased tensions in the region.

During the months of September and October 1941, several significant events occurred that would shape the course of World War II.

In September, the first use of gas chambers at the Auschwitz concentration camp took place. Over the next several years, millions of Jews, Roma, and others deemed undesirable by the Nazi regime would be killed in gas chambers at Auschwitz and other concentration camps.

In October, the Battle of Moscow began, with German forces launching a massive assault on the Soviet capital. Despite initial gains, the Germans were unable to capture Moscow and the battle ended in a stalemate. This was a significant setback for the Germans and marked the beginning of their retreat on the Eastern Front.

In December, Japan launched a surprise attack on the United States naval base at Pearl Harbor, drawing the US into the war. In response to the attack, President Franklin D. Roosevelt delivered a speech to Congress the next day, calling for a declaration of war against Japan. Congress responded by passing a declaration of war against Japan, officially entering the United States into World War II.

The decision to declare war on Japan was not without controversy, as many Americans were hesitant to enter the war. However, the attack on Pearl Harbor and the loss of American lives galvanized the country and made it clear that the US needed to take action to defend itself and its interests.

With the declaration of war, the US began mobilizing its military and industrial capabilities to support the war effort. This included ramping up production of weapons and other equipment, training new soldiers and sailors, and deploying troops to Europe and the Pacific to fight against the Axis powers.

In the Pacific, the United States launched its first major offensive of the war with the Doolittle Raid on Tokyo. This attack, carried out by B-25 bombers launched from an aircraft carrier, was a symbolic victory for the US but had little strategic impact on the war.

he year 1941 was a time of significant developments and innovations in the field of science and technology.

One of the most notable scientific innovations of 1941 was the development of the first electronic computer, called the Z3. This machine was designed by the German engineer Konrad Zuse, and it was capable of performing complex calculations and logical operations. The Z3 was a major breakthrough in the field of computing, and it laid the groundwork for many of the modern computers that we use today.

Another significant innovation of 1941 was the discovery of the nuclear fission process. This process, which involves the splitting of atomic nuclei, was first observed by the physicists Enrico Fermi and Leo Szilard in a laboratory at the University of Chicago. The discovery of fission opened the door to many new possibilities in the field of nuclear energy and paved the way for the development of the atomic bomb.

In addition, 1941 saw many other important scientific developments and innovations, including the first successful use of antibiotics to treat bacterial infections, the discovery of the structure of DNA, and the development of the first electronic television. These and other innovations helped to shape the world we live in today and have had a profound impact on science and technology.

During the month of August 1941, several important events took place around the world. In Europe, the war continued to escalate, with major battles taking place on the Eastern Front between the German and Soviet forces.

In the Pacific, the war also continued to escalate, as the Japanese continued their offensives against the Allied powers. In August, the Japanese captured Hong Kong and invaded the Dutch East Indies.

During the end of 1941, Germany was heavily involved in the ongoing conflict in Europe. The country had launched a massive invasion of the Soviet Union on June 22, 1941, in a campaign known as Operation Barbarossa. This was the largest military operation in history, involving more than three million German soldiers, as well as other Axis forces. The goal of the campaign was to defeat the Soviet Union and secure control of its vast resources.

Initially, the German invasion was successful, and the German forces quickly advanced deep into Soviet territory. However, the Soviet Union was able to mount a strong resistance, and the invasion eventually stalled. The harsh Russian winter also played a role, as it slowed the German advance and allowed the Soviet forces to regroup and counterattack. By the end of 1941, the German forces were struggling to maintain their positions in the face of strong Soviet resistance.

In addition, Germany was also facing increasing pressure from the Western Allies. On December 7, 1941, the Japanese launched a surprise attack on the American naval base at Pearl Harbor, which marked the United States' official entry into the war. This added a powerful new enemy to the German war effort, and it increased the pressure on the German forces.

Pt III

During the month of January 1942, several significant events took place around the world. In Europe, the war continued to escalate, with major battles taking place on the Eastern Front between the German and Soviet forces. The German invasion of the Soviet Union, which had begun on June 22, 1941, had stalled, and the Soviet forces were mounting a strong resistance.

In the Pacific, the war also continued to escalate. On January 2, 1942, the Japanese launched a major offensive in the Philippines, and they quickly captured the capital city of Manila. On January 11, they also captured the city of Kuala Lumpur in Malaya. The Japanese military was highly successful in these early campaigns, and they seemed to be on the verge of achieving their goals in the Pacific.

In America, the government implemented a number of measures to support the war effort. On January 16, 1942, the Office of War Mobilization was established, and on January 28, the Women's Army Corps was created. Many Americans also volunteered to serve in the military, and the country began to provide aid to the Allied powers. n February 1942, several significant events occurred that shaped the course of World War II. In the Pacific theater, the United States won a decisive victory over the Japanese at the Battle of the Java Sea. American and Dutch forces were able to sink several Japanese warships and successfully defend the Dutch East Indies.

This victory was a significant blow to Japanese ambitions in the region and marked a turning point in the war in the Pacific.

In Europe, the German army continued its advance deep into the Soviet Union. In a major offensive, German forces captured the city of Kharkov, a major industrial center in the Ukraine. The capture of Kharkov was a major victory for the Germans, but it also came at a heavy cost in terms of manpower and resources.

In North Africa, British forces under the command of General Bernard Montgomery launched a successful counterattack against the Germans at the Battle of Gazala. This battle was a turning point in the North African campaign, as the British were able to push the Germans out of Egypt and advance into Libya.

In the United States, President Franklin D. Roosevelt signed Executive Order 9066, authorizing the internment of Japanese Americans. This controversial decision was motivated by fear and racism and resulted in the forced relocation of more than 120,000 Japanese Americans to internment camps. This was a dark chapter in American history and is still remembered and condemned today.

n March 1942, several significant events occurred that shaped the course of World War II. In the Pacific theater, the Japanese continued their advance, capturing the island of New Guinea and the city of Rangoon in Burma. The capture of New Guinea was a major strategic victory for the Japanese, as it gave them control over a key location that could be used to launch further offensives against Australia. The capture of Rangoon, meanwhile, was a major blow to the British, as it cut off their supply lines to China and forced them to retreat to India.

In Europe, the German army launched a major offensive against the city of Leningrad, which would be besieged for nearly 900 days. The Siege of Leningrad was one of the longest and deadliest sieges in history, and it resulted in the deaths of hundreds of thousands of civilians. Despite the brutal conditions, the people of Leningrad held out against the German attackers, and the city eventually became a symbol of Soviet resistance to the Nazis.

In North Africa, British and German forces fought a series of battles in the Libyan desert, with the British eventually emerging victorious at the Battle of El Alamein. This battle was a turning point in the North African campaign, as it marked the end of the German advance and the beginning of the British counteroffensive. The victory at El Alamein paved the way for the eventual Allied liberation of North Africa and the opening of a second front against the Axis powers.

In the United States, President Roosevelt signed Executive Order 9102, establishing the War Relocation Authority to oversee the internment of Japanese Americans. This controversial decision was motivated by fear and racism, and it resulted in the forced relocation of more than 120,000 Japanese Americans to internment camps. The internment of Japanese Americans was a dark chapter in American history, and it is still remembered and condemned today.

In April 1942, several significant events occurred that shaped the course of World War II. In the Pacific theater, the Japanese continued their advance, capturing the island of Bataan in the Philippines. This victory allowed the Japanese to control the entrance to Manila Bay, a strategically important location. In Europe, the German army launched a major offensive against the city of Moscow, but was unable to capture the city and was eventually forced to retreat. In North Africa, British and German forces continued to fight a series of battles, with the British eventually emerging victorious at the Battle of Gazala.

In the United States, President Franklin D. Roosevelt signed Executive Order 9102, establishing the War Relocation Authority to oversee the internment of Japanese Americans. This controversial decision was motivated by fear and racism and resulted in the forced relocation of more than 120,000 Japanese Americans to internment camps. This was a dark chapter in American history and is still remembered and condemned today. In addition to these events, April 1942 was also marked by several significant cultural and social developments. In the United States, the song "White Christmas" by Irving Berlin was released and quickly became one of the most popular and enduring Christmas songs of all time. In the United Kingdom, the first Women's Auxiliary Air Force was established, allowing women to serve in non-combat roles in the British air force. In Germany, the Nazis began their deportation of Jews from the Warsaw Ghetto to the Treblinka extermination camp, as part of the Holocaust.

In June 1942, several significant events took place around the world, including the Battle of Midway, the start of the Normandy landings, and the execution of Anne Frank.

In the Pacific Theater of World War II, the Battle of Midway began on June 4th and lasted until June 7th. This was a decisive victory for the United States, as they were able to sink four Japanese aircraft carriers, severely damaging the Japanese navy. This battle is considered to be one of the most important in the Pacific Theater, as it marked a turning point in the war, with the United States gaining the upper hand over Japan.

On the Western Front, the Normandy landings, also known as D-Day, began on June 6th. This was a massive amphibious invasion by the Allied forces, consisting of British, Canadian, and American troops, on the beaches of Normandy, France. The invasion was a crucial step in the liberation of Europe from Nazi control, and is considered one of the most significant military operations in history. n response to the Nazi threat, the United States and the United Kingdom formed the Allies and began to plan a large-scale invasion of Europe in order to liberate the occupied territories and defeat the Axis powers. This invasion, known as D-Day, was a massive undertaking that required careful planning and coordination.

In the months leading up to D-Day, the Allies carried out a number of operations to prepare for the invasion. These included deception operations, such as the creation of a fake army in Kent, England, to distract the Germans from the real invasion force, and the destruction of key German defenses, such as radar stations and gun batteries, by air and naval raids.

On June 6th, 1944, the D-Day landings began, with British, Canadian, and American forces storming the beaches of Normandy, France. The invasion was successful, and marked a turning point in the war, with the Allies gaining a foothold in Europe and paving the way for their eventual victory.

Additionally, on June 12th, 1942, Anne Frank and her family were arrested by the Nazis and taken to the Westerbork transit camp in the Netherlands. Anne Frank, who was 13 years old at the time, would later become famous for her diary, which documented her experiences in the camp and her hopes for the future. She would ultimately perish in the Holocaust, but her diary would become a powerful testament to the atrocities of the war. July 1942 was a significant month in World War II, with several important events taking place around the world. In the Pacific Theater, the Battle of Savo Island began on July 7th, with the Japanese navy launching a surprise attack on Allied ships in the Solomon Islands. This was a major victory for the Japanese, who were able to sink four Allied cruisers and damage several others.

On the Eastern Front, the Battle of Rostov began on July 23rd, with the German army attempting to capture the city of Rostov-on-Don in the Soviet Union. The battle was a victory for the Germans, who were able to advance further into Soviet territory. However, the Soviet Union was able to regroup and launch a counterattack, eventually retaking the city in February 1943.

In the United States, the first rocket-powered aircraft, the Bell X-1, was successfully tested on July 16th. This marked a significant breakthrough in aviation technology, as the X-1 was the first aircraft to break the sound barrier.

Additionally, on July 20th, 1942, the Wannsee Conference was held in Berlin, Germany. This was a meeting of high-ranking Nazi officials, including Adolf Eichmann, who discussed the "Final Solution to the Jewish Question," or the plan to exterminate the Jewish population of Europe. This conference marked the beginning of the systematic extermination of Jews in concentration camps during the Holocaust.

August 1942 was a significant month in World War II, with several important events taking place around the world. In the Pacific Theater, the Guadalcanal campaign began on August 7th, with the United States launching an amphibious assault on the island of Guadalcanal in the Solomon Islands. This was the first major Allied offensive in the Pacific, and marked the beginning of a long and grueling campaign to retake the island from the Japanese.

On the Eastern Front, the Battle of Stalingrad began on August 23rd, with the German army launching a massive assault on the Soviet city of Stalingrad. This would become one of the most brutal and devastating battles of the war, with heavy casualties on both sides. The battle would ultimately end in a Soviet victory in February 1943, marking a turning point in the war on the Eastern Front.

In the United States, on August 12th, the first successful test of the atomic bomb was conducted at the Los Alamos laboratory in New Mexico. This marked a major breakthrough in nuclear technology, and would ultimately lead to the development of the first atomic bombs used in warfare.

Additionally, on August 22nd, 1942, the Quit India Movement was launched by the Indian National Congress, calling for the British to immediately grant India independence. This sparked widespread protests and civil disobedience across India, leading to a crackdown by the British authorities. The movement ultimately failed to achieve its goals, but it did help to pave the way for India's eventual independence in 1947.

September 1942 was a significant month in World War II, with several important events taking place around the world. In the Pacific Theater, the Battle of Milne Bay began on September 25th, with the Allies launching an amphibious assault on the Japanese-occupied island of New Guinea. This was the first time that the Japanese had been defeated in a land battle in the Pacific and marked a turning point in the war.

On the Eastern Front, the Battle of Rzhev began on September 30th, with the Soviet Union launching a major offensive against the German army in the region of Rzhev. This was a brutal and costly battle, with heavy casualties on both sides, but ultimately ended in a Soviet victory.

In the United States, on September 15th, the first black pilots in the United States Army Air Corps, known as the Tuskegee Airmen, were trained at Tuskegee University in Alabama. This marked a significant milestone in the fight for racial equality in the United States, as the Tuskegee Airmen would go on to serve with distinction in World War II.

Additionally, on September 29th, 1942, the British Eighth Army, under the command of General Bernard Montgomery, launched a successful attack on the German-occupied city of El Alamein in Egypt. This marked the beginning of the end for German forces in North Africa and paved the way for the Allies to push into Italy and the rest of Europe.

October 1942 was a significant month in World War II, with several important events taking place around the world. In the Pacific Theater, the

Battle of Cape Esperance began on October 11th, with the United States and Japan engaging in a naval battle off the coast of Guadalcanal. This was a victory for the United States, who were able to sink several Japanese ships and halt their advance in the region.

On the Eastern Front, the Battle of Moscow began on October 2nd, with the German army launching a massive offensive against the Soviet Union in an attempt to capture the city of Moscow. This would become one of the most important and decisive battles of the war, with the Soviet Union ultimately pushing the Germans back and preventing them from taking the city.

In the United States, on October 14th, the first flight of the B-29 Superfortress, the largest and most advanced bomber of its time, took place. This marked a major milestone in aviation technology, and the B-29 would go on to play a key role in the war, conducting bombing raids against Japanese cities.

Additionally, on October 27th, 1942, the British Eighth Army, under the command of General Bernard Montgomery, launched a major offensive against the German and Italian forces at El Alamein in Egypt. This was a decisive victory for the Allies, who were able to drive the Axis powers out of Egypt and pave the way for their advance into Libya and Tunisia.

In November 1942, a number of momentous events occurred in the midst of World War II. In the Pacific Theater, the ongoing Battle of Guadalcanal continued to rage, with the United States and Japanese forces locked in a fierce struggle for control of the strategically important island. Meanwhile, on the Eastern Front, the Soviet Union launched a massive counteroffensive against the German army, pushing them back from Moscow and retaking several key cities. This marked the beginning of the end for German forces on the Eastern Front, as the Soviets began to gain the upper hand in the war.

In the United States, the top-secret Manhattan Project, which aimed to develop the world's first atomic bombs, was officially established on November 16th. This marked the beginning of a massive effort to develop the technology needed to build and deliver atomic bombs, which would ultimately be used against Japan in 1945.

Additionally, on November 8th, the Allies launched Operation Torch, an invasion of North Africa aimed at pushing the Axis powers out of the region. The operation involved British, American, and French forces landing in Morocco and Algeria, and was a crucial step in the liberation of Europe, as it allowed the Allies to open up a second front in the war.

Part 3: January - February 1943

January 1943 was a significant month in World War II, with several important events taking place around the world. In the Pacific Theater, the Battle of Guadalcanal continued, with the United States and Japanese forces continuing to clash on the island. However, by the end of the month, the Americans had secured control of the island, marking a major victory and a turning point in the war in the Pacific.

On the Eastern Front, the Soviet Union continued its counteroffensive against the German army, pushing them back and reclaiming several key cities. This marked the beginning of the end for German forces on the Eastern Front, as the Soviets began to gain the upper hand in the war.

In the United States, the top-secret Manhattan Project continued to progress, with scientists working around the clock to develop the world's first atomic bombs. Additionally, on January 24th, the first American bomber raid on Berlin took place, with the United States beginning to carry out strategic bombing campaigns against Germany.

February 1943 came around with several important events taking place around the world. In the Pacific Theater, the Battle of Guadalcanal officially came to an end on February 9th, with the United States securing control of the island. This marked a major victory for the Allies and a turning point in the war in the Pacific.

On the Eastern Front, the Soviet Union continued its counteroffensive against the German army, pushing them back and reclaiming several key cities. This marked the beginning of the end for German forces on the Eastern Front, as the Soviets began to gain the upper hand in the war.

In the United States, the top-secret Manhattan Project continued to progress, with scientists working around the clock to develop the world's first atomic bombs. Additionally, on February 23rd, the United States launched a major air raid on the German city of Schweinfurt, targeting the city's ball bearing factories. This marked the beginning of a sustained bombing campaign against Germany's industrial capabilities.

In March 1943, the tide of World War II continued to turn in favor of the Allies. In the Pacific Theater, the United States launched a major offensive against the Japanese-held island of New Georgia, kicking off a grueling campaign to retake the Solomon Islands from the Japanese. Meanwhile, on the Eastern Front, the Soviet Union continued its counteroffensive against the German army, pushing them back and reclaiming several key cities.

Back in the United States, the top-secret Manhattan Project chugged along, with scientists working around the clock to develop the world's first atomic bombs. And on March 9th, American bombers launched a massive raid on the German city of Frankfurt, targeting its industrial capabilities in a bid to cripple the Nazi war machine.

Between January and March 1943, several significant scientific discoveries were made. In January, the first successful self-sustaining nuclear chain reaction was achieved at the University of Chicago, marking a major milestone in the development of atomic weaponry. In February, the first successful extraction of pure penicillin was achieved, paving the way for the mass production of antibiotics. And in March, the first successful test of an American-made jet aircraft, the Bell XP-59A, took place, marking a major milestone in aviation technology. Overall, these discoveries played a crucial role in the advancement of science and technology during World War II.

April 1943 was a significant month in World War II, with several important events taking place around the world. In the Pacific Theater, the United States continued its offensive against the Japanese-held island of New Georgia, ultimately securing control of the island by the end of the month. This marked a major victory for the Allies and a significant blow to Japanese forces in the Pacific.

On the Eastern Front, the Soviet Union continued its counteroffensive against the German army, pushing them back and reclaiming several key cities. This marked the beginning of the end for German forces on the Eastern Front, as the Soviets began to gain the upper hand in the war.

In the United States, the top-secret Manhattan Project continued to progress, with scientists working around the clock to develop the world's first atomic bombs. Additionally, on April 19th, American forces launched a major air raid on the German city of Ploesti, targeting the city's oil fields and refineries. This marked the beginning of a sustained bombing campaign against Germany's oil production capabilities. May 1943 was a significant month in World War II, with several important events taking place around the world. In the Pacific Theater, the United States continued its offensive against Japanese-held islands, with the goal of securing control of the region. This marked the beginning of a long and grueling campaign to retake the Solomon Islands from the Japanese.

On the Eastern Front, the Soviet Union continued its counteroffensive against the German army, pushing them back and reclaiming several key cities. This marked the beginning of the end for German forces on the Eastern Front, as the Soviets began to gain the upper hand in the war.

In the United States, the top-secret Manhattan Project continued to progress, with scientists working around the clock to develop the world's first atomic bombs. Additionally, on May 27th, the United States launched a major air raid on the German city of Wilhelmshaven, targeting the city's naval base and shipbuilding facilities. This marked the beginning of a sustained bombing campaign against Germany's naval capabilities. June 1943 was a significant month in World War II, with several important events taking place around the world. In the Pacific Theater, the United States continued its offensive against Japanese-held islands, with the goal of securing control of the region. This marked the beginning of a long and grueling campaign to retake the Solomon Islands from the Japanese.

On the Eastern Front, the Soviet Union continued its counteroffensive against the German army, pushing them back and reclaiming several key cities. This marked the beginning of the end for German forces on the Eastern Front, as the Soviets began to gain the upper hand in the war.

In the United States, the top-secret Manhattan Project continued to progress, with scientists working around the clock to develop the world's first atomic bombs. Additionally, on June 4th, the United States launched a major air raid on the German city of Münster, targeting the city's industrial capabilities. This marked the beginning of a sustained bombing campaign against Germany's industrial heartland, as the United States sought to cripple the Nazi war machine.

Meanwhile, on the Western Front, the Allies began to prepare for the invasion of Europe, with the goal of liberating occupied territories and opening up a second front in the war. This operation, known as Operation Overlord, was one of the largest and most complex military operations in history, and would eventually lead to the liberation of Europe and the end of the war. . In 1943, the war in the Pacific continued to rage on, with significant developments and intense fighting taking place throughout the year. In the early months of the year, the United States launched a major offensive against the Japanese-held island of New Georgia, ultimately securing control of the island in a major victory for the Allies.

Meanwhile, in the Solomon Islands, the United States continued its campaign to retake the islands from the Japanese, launching a series of amphibious assaults on key Japanese-held positions. This marked the beginning of a long and grueling campaign to push the Japanese out of the Solomon Islands, with heavy fighting taking place on the islands of Guadalcanal, Tulagi, and Rendova.

In May, the United States launched a major air raid on the Japanese naval base at Rabaul, targeting the base's airfields and shipping facilities. This marked the beginning of a sustained bombing campaign against Japanese naval and air capabilities in the Pacific, as the United States sought to weaken the Japanese war effort.

By the end of the year, the tide of the war in the Pacific had begun to turn in favor of the Allies, with the United States making significant gains against the Japanese. However, the war was far from over, and the fighting in the Pacific would continue for several more years before the Allies were able to secure a final victory. On the Eastern Front, the Soviet Union continued its counteroffensive against the German army, pushing them back and reclaiming several key cities. This marked the beginning of the end for German forces on the Eastern Front, as the Soviets began to gain the upper hand in the war.

In the United States, the top-secret Manhattan Project continued to progress, with scientists working around the clock to develop the world's first atomic bombs. Additionally, on July 5th, the United States launched a major air raid on the German city of Hamburg, targeting the city's industrial capabilities. This marked the beginning of a sustained bombing campaign against Germany's industrial heartland, as the United States sought to cripple the Nazi war machine.

Meanwhile, on the Western Front, the Allies continued to prepare for the invasion of Europe, with the goal of liberating occupied territories and opening up a second front in the war. This operation, known as Operation Overlord, was one of the largest and most complex military operations in history, and would eventually lead to the liberation of Europe and the end of the war.

August 1943 was a significant month in World War II, with several important events and developments taking place around the world. In the Pacific Theater, the United States continued its offensive against Japanese-held islands, with the goal of securing control of the region. This marked the beginning of a long and grueling campaign to retake the Solomon Islands from the Japanese.

On the Eastern Front, the Soviet Union continued its counteroffensive against the German army, pushing them back and reclaiming several key cities. This marked the beginning of the end for German forces on the Eastern Front, as the Soviets began to gain the upper hand in the war. In particular, on August 23rd, the Soviet Union launched a major offensive against the city of Kharkov, successfully retaking the city after a month of intense fighting.

In the United States, the top-secret Manhattan Project continued to progress, with scientists working around the clock to develop the world's first atomic bombs. Additionally, on August 1st, the United States launched a major air raid on the German city of Peenemunde, targeting the city's experimental rocket facility. This marked the beginning of a sustained bombing campaign against Germany's weapons research facilities, as the United States sought to cripple the Nazi war machine.

Meanwhile, on the Western Front, the Allies continued to prepare for the invasion of Europe, with the goal of liberating occupied territories and opening up a second front in the war. This operation, known as Operation Overlord, was one of the largest and most complex military operations in history, and would eventually lead to the liberation of Europe and the end of the war.

1943 was a significant year for scientific development, with several important discoveries and advancements taking place around the world.

One of the most significant scientific developments of the year was the continued progress of the top-secret Manhattan Project in the United States. Scientists working on the project were racing against time to develop the world's first atomic bombs, and by the end of the year, they had made significant progress in their efforts.

Additionally, 1943 saw the discovery of several important new drugs and medical treatments. In the United States, researchers at the University of Wisconsin-Madison successfully synthesized penicillin, paving the way for the widespread use of the life-saving antibiotic. And in the United Kingdom, scientists at Oxford University discovered the structure of DNA, marking a major breakthrough in the field of genetics.

Overall, 1943 was a significant year for scientific development, with several important discoveries and advancements taking place around the world. These developments would have a profound impact on the world, shaping the course of history and improving the lives of countless people.

Chapter 9: 1944

In the Pacific Theater, the United States continued its offensive against Japanese-held islands, with the goal of securing control of the region. This marked the beginning of a long and grueling campaign to push the Japanese out of the Solomon Islands, with heavy fighting taking place on the islands of Bougainville, Choiseul, and Treasury.

On the Eastern Front, the Soviet Union continued its counteroffensive against the German army, pushing them back and reclaiming several key cities. This marked the beginning of the end for German forces on the Eastern Front, as the Soviets began to gain the upper hand in the war. In particular, on January 27th, the Soviet Union launched a major offensive against the city of Leningrad, finally lifting the nearly 900-day-long Siege of Leningrad.

January 1944 -

The first month of 1944 was a turbulent one, with Allied forces continuing to make gains against the Axis powers. In the East, the Soviet Red Army began a major offensive against the German forces in Leningrad and

Novgorod, pushing them back and allowing the siege of the two cities to be lifted. The Red Army also launched an offensive against the Germans in the Ukraine, pushing them back towards the Carpathian Mountains.

Meanwhile, in the West, the Allies continued to make gains in Italy. In January, they captured Monte Cassino, a strategic mountain stronghold that had long been held by the Germans. This victory allowed the Allies to move closer to Rome, which would be captured in June.

In the Pacific, the Allies continued their island-hopping campaign, with the Marines capturing Kwajalein Atoll in the Marshall Islands. This was a major victory that cleared the way for the Allies to attack the Japanese stronghold of Truk.

February 1944 -

February saw the Allies continuing to make advances against the Axis powers. In the East, the Red Army scored major victories in Leningrad and Ukraine, pushing the Germans back further and further. In the West, the Allies captured Anzio,

The second half of WWII began when the Allies launched the invasion of Normandy on June 6, 1944, which marked the beginning of the liberation of Western Europe from Nazi Germany. The Allies then continued to fight their way across Europe and in August, the Allies liberated Paris.

In the Atlantic, the Allies achieved a major victory when they broke the German U-boat codes in 1943. This allowed them to track and destroy the German submarines, which were a major threat to Allied shipping.

In the Pacific, the Allies continued their island-hopping campaign against Japan, launching air raids and amphibious assaults on Japanese-held islands.

n particular, on June 22nd, the Soviet Union launched a major offensive against the city of Kiev, successfully retaking the city after a month of intense fighting.

The second half of 1944 saw the Allies continue to gain ground in their battles against the Axis Powers. In July, the Allies launched Operation

Cobra, a major offensive in Normandy, which resulted in the liberation of most of Northern France. In August, the Allies entered Paris, which had been occupied by the Germans since 1940. In September, the Allies pushed through the Siegfried Line and advanced into Germany. In the east, the Soviet Red Army continued to make advances against the Germans, and in December the Soviets retook their capital of Moscow.

Meanwhile, in the Pacific, the Allies continued to push back the Japanese. In October, they launched the Battle of Leyte Gulf, which resulted in the largest naval battle in history. The Allies also recaptured the Philippines and invaded Okinawa in April 1945. In addition to military successes, the second half of 1944 also saw a number of other important events. The Bretton Woods Conference was held in July, which established the International Monetary Fund and the World Bank. In August, the United Nations was formed. And in October, the first Allied troops landed in the Philippines.

The first half of 1945 saw the end of World War II in Europe as the Allies pushed back Nazi Germany from all fronts. In January, the Red Army finally liberated the Auschwitz concentration camp in Poland, and in April, the Allies took Berlin and Hitler committed suicide.

The Pacific War dragged on, however, as the United States and its allies continued to fight Japanese forces in the Philippines, Iwo Jima, Okinawa, and elsewhere. In July, the United States detonated the first atomic bomb over Hiroshima, Japan, and followed up with a second atomic bomb over Nagasaki a few days later. The Japanese surrendered in August, ending the war.

The second half of 1945 was a time of great upheaval and change, as World War II came to an end and the world began to rebuild from the devastating conflict.

In Europe, the final months of the war saw the liberation of the concentration camps and the end of the Holocaust, as well as the surrender of Nazi Germany and the beginning of the Nuremberg trials. In the Pacific, the United States dropped atomic bombs on the Japanese cities of Hiroshima and Nagasaki, leading to Japan's surrender and the end of the war.

As the dust settled, the international community began to grapple with the aftermath of the war and the difficult task of rebuilding. The United Nations was founded in October 1945, and countries around the world began to develop plans for post-war reconstruction and peacekeeping.

Meanwhile, in the United States, President Harry Truman faced the challenges of demobilizing the military and transitioning the country back to a peacetime economy. The GI Bill was passed, providing education and job training for returning veterans, and the country experienced a period of economic growth and prosperity.

World War II was a time of rapid technological advancement, as various nations sought to gain an edge over their enemies on the battlefield.

One of the most significant technological breakthroughs of the war was the development of jet aircraft. The Germans were the first to field jet fighters, with the introduction of the Messerschmitt Me 262 in 1944. The Allies soon followed suit, with the British developing the Gloster Meteor and the Americans producing the Lockheed P-80 Shooting Star. Jet aircraft allowed for faster, more agile dogfighting and gave pilots a critical advantage in combat.

Another major technological development was the creation of the first electronic computers. The Germans developed the Z3, the world's first programmable computer, while the British built the Colossus, a machine used to crack German codes. The Americans, meanwhile, developed the ENIAC, the first general-purpose electronic computer, which was used for a wide range of applications, including weather prediction and nuclear weapons research.

In addition, the war saw the widespread use of radar for the first time, allowing for more effective air defense and naval warfare. The Germans also developed the first operational guided missiles, with the V-1 and V-2 rockets, which were used to bomb targets in England and Belgium.

Overall, World War II was a time of rapid technological advancement, with numerous breakthroughs that would lay the groundwork for future innovations and greatly impact the course of the war

www.ingramcontent.com/pod-product-compliance
Lightning Source LLC
La Vergne TN
LVHW050342160826
845677LV00014B/3743

* 9 7 9 8 3 6 9 9 1 1 5 2 5 *